KING
DAVID

Trusting God
for a Lifetime

ROBBIE CASTLEMAN

FISHERMAN
BIBLE STUDY SERIES

King David

PUBLISHED BY WATERBROOK PRESS

12265 Oracle Blvd., Suite 200

Colorado Springs, Colorado 80921

A division of Random House, Inc.

ISBN 0-87788-165-0

Printed in the United States of America

2006

10 9 8 7 6 5

Contents

How to Use This Studyguide

Fisherman studyguides are based on the inductive approach to Bible study. Inductive study is discovery study; we discover what the Bible says as we ask questions about its content and search for answers. This is quite different from the process in which a teacher *tells* a group *about* the Bible—what it means and what to do about it. In inductive study, God speaks directly to each of us through his Word.

A group functions best when a leader keeps the discussion on target, but the leader is neither the teacher nor the "answer person." A leader's responsibility is to *ask*—not *tell*. The answers come from the text itself as group members examine, discuss, and think together about the passage.

There are four kinds of questions in each study. The first is an *approach question*. Asked and answered before the Bible passage is read, this question breaks the ice and helps you start thinking about the topic of the Bible study. It begins to reveal where thoughts and feelings need to be transformed by Scripture.

Some of the earlier questions in each study are *observation questions*—who, what, where, when, and how—designed to help you learn some basic facts about the passage of Scripture.

Once you know what the Bible says, you need to ask, *What does it mean?* These *interpretation questions* help you discover the writer's basic message.

Next come *application questions,* which ask, *What does it mean to me?* They challenge you to live out the Scripture's life-transforming message.

Fisherman studyguides provide spaces between questions for jotting down responses as well as any related questions you would like to raise in the group. Each group member should have a copy of the studyguide and may take a turn in leading the group.

A group should use any accurate, modern translation of the Bible such as the *New International Version,* the *New American Standard Bible,* the *New Living Translation,* the *New Revised Standard Version,* the *New Jerusalem Bible,* or the *Good News Bible.* (Other translations or paraphrases of the Bible may be referred to when additional help is needed.) Bible commentaries should not be brought to a Bible study because they tend to dampen discussion and keep people from thinking for themselves.

Suggestions for Group Leaders

1. Thoroughly read and study the Bible passage before the meeting. Get a firm grasp on its themes and begin applying its teachings for yourself. Pray that the Holy Spirit will "guide you into all truth" (John 16:13) so that your leadership will guide others.

2. If any of the studyguide's questions seem ambiguous or unnatural to you, rephrase them, feeling free to add others that seem necessary to bring out the meaning of a verse.

3. Begin (and end) the study promptly. Start by asking someone to pray that every participant will both understand the passage and be open to its transforming power. Remember, the Holy Spirit is the teacher, not you!

4. Ask for volunteers to read the passages aloud.

5. As you ask the studyguide's questions in sequence, encourage everyone to participate in the discussion. If some are silent, try gently suggesting, "Let's have an answer from someone who hasn't spoken up yet."

6. If a question comes up that you can't answer, don't be afraid to admit that you're baffled. Assign the topic as a research project for someone to report on next week, or say, "I'll do some studying and let you know what I find out."

7. Keep the discussion moving, but be sure it stays focused. Though a certain number of tangents are inevitable, you'll want to quickly bring the discussion back to the topic at hand. Also, learn to pace the discussion so that you finish the lesson in the time allotted.

8. Don't be afraid of silences; some questions take time to answer, and some people need time to gather courage to speak. If silence persists, rephrase your question, but resist the temptation to answer it yourself.

9. If someone comes up with an answer that is clearly illogical or unbiblical, ask for further clarification: "What verse suggests that to you?"

10. Discourage overuse of cross references. Learn all you can from the passage at hand, while selectively incorporating a few important references suggested in the studyguide.

11. Some questions are marked with a ✐. This indicates that further information is available in the Leader's Notes at the back of the guide.

12. For further information on getting a new Bible study group started and keeping it functioning effectively, read *You Can Start a Bible Study Group* by Gladys Hunt and *Pilgrims in Progress: Growing Through Groups* by Jim and Carol Plueddemann. (Both books are available from Shaw Books).

Suggestions for Group Members

1. Learn and apply the following ground rules for effective Bible study. (If new members join the group later, review these guidelines with the whole group.)

2. Remember that your goal is to learn all that you can *from the Bible passage being studied.* Let it speak for itself without using Bible commentaries or other Bible passages. There is more than enough in each assigned passage to keep your group productively occupied for one session. Sticking to the passage saves the group from insecurity ("I don't have the right reference books—or the time to read anything else.") and confusion ("Where did *that* come from? I thought we were studying _____.").

3. Avoid the temptation to bring up those fascinating tangents that don't really grow out of the passage you are discussing. If the topic is of common interest, you can bring it up later in informal conversation after the study. Meanwhile, help one another stick to the subject.

4. Encourage one another to participate. People remember best what they discover and verbalize

for themselves. Some people are naturally shy, while others may be afraid of making a mistake. If your discussion is free and friendly and you show real interest in what other group members think and feel, the quieter ones will be more likely to speak up. Remember, the more people involved in a discussion, the richer it will be.

5. Guard yourself from answering too many questions or talking too much. Give others a chance to share their ideas. If you are one who participates easily, discipline yourself by counting to ten before you open your mouth.

6. Make personal, honest applications and commit yourself to letting God's Word change you.

Introduction

From the time the teenage shepherd David was anointed king until the day he was crowned king of Israel at thirty-seven years of age, God had been training David for his specific purposes. Like an athlete training for a marathon, David found the preparation demanding, challenging, and lengthy.

As a shepherd, David learned to trust God for his safety, and he developed the compassion he needed to be a shepherd over Israel (1 Samuel 17:34-37). As a young warrior, David was jealous for the God of Israel, and his bravery made him a national hero (1 Samuel 18:7). Serving as a musician to the volatile and unpredictable King Saul, David gained an understanding of this king who would continually threaten his life, and he learned to respond with mercy (1 Samuel 24:10). For nearly ten years as a fugitive, David experienced God's protection and deliverance. Through his mistakes, disappointments, and fear, David learned to trust God's perfect and patient timing. As a leader of hundreds of distressed, indebted, and discontented men, David grew to be a man of wise discernment and shrewd politics (1 Samuel 22:2). Finally, having completed his training, David was crowned king of Israel.

In this study we'll see how King David handled the pressures of success. Often he did well, sometimes he did poorly, but through it all, David continued to grow as a man "after [God's] own heart" (1 Samuel 13:14). It took guidance, rebuke, patience, forgiveness, and discipline. And it took time.

In an age of fast food and automatic banking, we can easily grow impatient and long for quick success as we struggle to become people after God's own heart. But God is not in the business of turning out "instant" disciples. Training obedient, trusting followers takes time, and time is God's specialty. It is my prayer that you, like David, will learn how to trust God more in the process of life and will grow in obedience and patience. "He who began a good work in you will carry it on to completion until the day of Christ Jesus" (Philippians 1:6).

Is My Worship Genuine?

2 SAMUEL 6

Scottish historian Thomas Carlyle once observed, "What greater calamity can befall a nation than the loss of worship?" For individuals as well as nations, understanding and acknowledging a power greater than our own is necessary for peace and hope. Losing sight of God leaves us with only ourselves, which can lead to hardheartedness, confusion, and pride.

This is the very situation in which we find the Israelites. For years the people have followed Saul, and they have payed more attention to him than to God's Law. Now David has been crowned king, and he realizes that something important is missing and that he must do something to pull the kingdom together. The independent tribes of Israel must once again learn how to truly worship God together as the nation of Israel.

1. Describe your personal commitment to worship.

READ 2 SAMUEL 6:1-11.

⁊ 2. To fully unify Israel under God's authority, David recognized the need to bring the ark to his new strategic capital, Jerusalem. What did the ark signify for Israel?

3. In Numbers 4:15 and 7:9, God gave instructions to Moses that the Levitical priests were to carry the ark on poles on their shoulders, and he warned that touching the ark would result in death. What did the people's disregard for or ignorance of this procedure indicate about their attitude toward the Law at this time? toward worship?

4. Why was Uzzah's action irreverent?

⁊ *Indicates further information in Leader's Notes*

5. Why was David angry and afraid?

   If you had been in David's situation, how would
   you have reacted to this event?

6. What did David's decision to leave the ark with
   Obed-Edom reveal about his character?

READ 2 SAMUEL 6:12-23.

7. To see how David transported the ark the second
   time, read 1 Chronicles 15:11-15. What had David
   learned?

⚲ 8. How did David express his gladness? Describe the celebration.

9. Give at least two possible reasons for Michal's attitude toward David and her reaction to his dancing before the Lord.

10. What does David's reply tell us about his attitude toward Michal? toward God? toward himself?

11. In what ways did David give himself and forget himself in an expression of genuine worship?

How is this different from "getting something from the service"?

12. Describe some of the obstacles, within yourself and outside yourself, that keep you from worshiping God with your whole heart. What can you do to overcome these obstacles?

David wrote Psalm 24 for this special occasion. Read this psalm aloud together. Use it to share in David's joy and to express your own heartfelt worship to God.

Do I See from God's Perspective?

2 SAMUEL 7

How often do we run ahead of God and decide what should happen in our lives? Sometimes out of zeal, sometimes out of fear, we charge ahead with our agendas and then feel disillusioned or angry when things don't turn out the way we had planned.

David experienced a similar desire to make something happen. He wanted to honor God in a specific way, a way that seemed good and right. As he became aware of God's perspective on the matter, he learned that God's sovereign plans are better in the long run.

1. Describe a time in your life when you were disappointed that your efforts did not turn out the way you had planned.

READ 2 SAMUEL 7:1-17.

    ✒ 2.   What idea did David share with Nathan?

             What motivated David?

    ✒ 3.   Why might God not have wanted a house? (Hint: Think about how it would have influenced the Israelites' concept of who he was.)

    4.   What time periods of David's life did God address? What did he say about each?

✐ 5. Summarize briefly God's response to David's idea in verses 5-16. How do you think David felt when he heard that God wasn't excited about his idea?

How would God's reply concerning David's future have helped him accept God's plans for a house?

READ 2 SAMUEL 7:18-29.

6. As David entered God's presence, what was his attitude toward himself?

What does the name with which David addressed God reveal about his attitude toward God?

7. What did David see as the reason for God's goodness toward him?

8. In what ways did David describe the uniqueness of his God? In what ways was Israel unique?

9. What did David ask God to do? Why?

10. How did David's reverence for God, his remembrance of God's faithfulness, and his reliance on God's Word help him as he faced his disappointment about God's different plans for building a house?

11. With what attitudes do you sometimes come before God in prayer?

In what ways can your attitudes toward God and toward yourself influence the effectiveness of your prayers?

12. What specific things can you do to recall God's faithfulness to you as you pray?

13. How can relying on God's Word help you when you pray?

What specific actions would help you rely more on the truth of God's Word in prayer?

Do I Act with Justice and Righteousness?

2 SAMUEL 8–10

Being a man of his times, David led his share of battles to protect and enlarge his kingdom. But the foundation of David's reign was his faith in God and his knowledge that God was with him and the people of Israel. Because of this conviction, he could respond aggressively when necessary and with kindness when it was right.

In our day, as it was in David's, it is a challenge to rely on God and to act justly.

The chapters covered in this study focus on the zenith of David's kingship. All of the wars that took place during David's reign are catalogued in chapter 8, and a particularly significant and perilous war is detailed in chapter 10. Between these two chapters that describe David's international importance and military prowess, is the story of his tender, thoughtful dealings with his friend Jonathan's lame son.

1. Describe a time when you succeeded at something. On what or whom did you rely for success?

READ 2 SAMUEL 8.

2. Summarize David's far-reaching accomplishments. What do verses 6, 11, and 14 reveal about David's perspective on power and success?

⚘ 3. What qualities characterized David's reign (verse 15)?

What do you know of David's past that would contribute to the presence of these qualities?

4. Identify specific situations in your life now that need to be handled with the godly characteristics of justice and righteousness. Consider family issues as well as activities and business outside the home.

READ 2 SAMUEL 9.

✐5. At the height of his power, whom did David seek out? Why?

6. What do you think Mephibosheth might have thought and felt when he was called to meet David?

7. What words did Mephibosheth use to describe himself in verse 8? What negative effect might Mephibosheth's handicap have had on his self-image?

8. Describe a time when you, like Mephibosheth, have felt unworthy of grace and unmerited favor. In what ways does David's response parallel God's response to undeserving people?

9. What specific steps can you take as an individual, a group, or a church to find those to whom you may "show God's kindness" (verses 3-4)?

10. How did David's kindness to Mephibosheth illustrate justice and righteousness?

In practical terms, discuss the challenge of loving those who are handicapped physically, emotionally, and mentally.

READ 2 SAMUEL 10.

11. What was David's apparent motivation in dealing kindly with others?

Contrast the response of the Ammonites to David's kindness with that of Mephibosheth. How do you account for the difference?

12. The war described in verses 6-14 was fought by hired soldiers from Aramea (Syria) to bolster the Ammonite forces against Israel. What attitude did Joab have toward Israel? toward God?

13. What effect would David's presence in the second battle have had on the morale of the soldiers and of the entire country?

   How did David's presence on the battlefield demonstrate his continuing reliance on the Lord?

14. What do your actions reveal about your reliance on God?

Do I Face My Sin?

2 SAMUEL 11:1–12:25

S in is very rarely a single act but is "like a rope twined from many threads…one [sin] grows out of another, and often the new is committed to cover or excuse the old" (Gotthold). It is not surprising, then, that our inclination to defend and protect ourselves when we sin is as natural to us as breathing. Even a great king and mighty warrior like David was human and was susceptible to temptation and prone to covering up his wrongs. The scriptural account in this study shows us not only the "many threads" of David's sin but also the healing forgiveness of God.

1. How do you tend to respond if you are caught doing something wrong?

READ 2 SAMUEL 11.

2. How did David's actions that evening in Jerusalem indicate that he lacked something constructive to do? Where should David have been? (Recall David's activities in 2 Samuel 10:17-18.)

3. What verbs in verses 2-4 show the progression of David's lust?

In what ways were David's emotions, mind, and will involved in his sin?

4. Discuss ways to "nip in the bud" the temptations of life before they lead you to make sinful decisions. Consider a variety of real-life temptations, and be practical in your suggestions for resisting them.

5. What was David's first action after he heard that Bathsheba was pregnant (verse 8)?

What was Uriah's response to David in verse 11? Why did he respond this way?

6. Contrast David's behavior toward his enemy Saul in 1 Samuel 24:10 with his behavior toward his dedicated soldier Uriah. What made the difference?

7. Why do you think it comforted David to rationalize Uriah's death?

8. Why does one sin often lead to another?

In what ways can an understanding of the nature of sin help you resist temptation?

Secure in the cover-up of his sin, David married Bathsheba and went about conducting the affairs of state. Nearly one year passed between the end of chapter 11 and the beginning of chapter 12.

Read 2 Samuel 12:1-25.

9. Why was the parable of the poor man's ewe lamb appropriate and effective for showing David his sin?

Why did David respond so strongly to the parable?

10. List the things that God had done and would do for David (verses 7-12).

How did God's two judgments correspond to David's sins of adultery and murder?

11. What was the root of David's sin?

Describe the tone and content of David's reply to God's judgment.

12. Summarize David's mood and actions before and after the death of his child. What was David's apparent motivation? What did David's reply to his servants in verse 22 reveal about his dependence upon God?

13. How did God communicate his forgiveness to David through the prophet Nathan when Bathsheba gave birth to a second child (see verse 25)?

14. If you can, share an experience you've had that demonstrates both God's justice and his love to you.

Can I Rejoice?

PSALM 32

S in. It pervades our lives. It causes us to hurt others and others to hurt us. It damages relationships, destroys life, and steals joy. This psalm, written by David as he faced the glaring sin in his own life, shows us that whenever we are willing to uncover our sins, God is willing to cover us with his forgiveness and give us new reasons to rejoice.

1. Can you rejoice in the Lord right now? Why or why not?

↗ READ PSALM 32.

2. Who is blessed in verses 1-2?

How are transgression and sin forgiven and covered? (See Ephesians 2:1-5; Romans 5:6-11; and Colossians 1:19-23.)

3. What impact did unconfessed sin have on David's life?

Describe a time when you have felt God's heavy hand in a similar way.

4. What happened when David acknowledged his sin?

5. What did David recommend in verses 6-7 for people who want to identify themselves with God?

6. What kind of "trouble" was David referring to in verse 7? What kind of trouble do you experience?

✑ 7. What truth is conveyed by the repeated similar verbs in verse 8?

What instruction and counsel has God given you?

8. According to the negative example in verse 9, what characteristics prevent a person from following God's instruction?

9. Compare the results of obeying and disobeying God's teaching in verse 10.

When have you experienced either of these results?

10. How is verse 11 a result of verse 5?

11. In your life, what have you experienced as a result of confessing your sins and trusting God?

How Can I Best Love My Family?

2 SAMUEL 14; LUKE 15:11-24

David's extended family made for some complex relationships. In 2 Samuel 13, we see the sins of the father repeated by his sons when Amnon, David's eldest son, raped his stepsister, Tamar. Tamar's full brother Absalom shrewdly orchestrated the murder of Amnon to avenge the violation of his sister. Afterward Absalom fled to take refuge with his mother's father.

David was angry at these events, but he did not administer the required penalties for rape and murder. Whether David was motivated by self-conscious guilt because of his own history of lust and murder or by leniency wrongly intended as forgiveness and grace, the consequences of his inaction nearly cost him his throne and his life.

1. If you were David, what would you have felt during the three years of Absalom's exile? In your response, consider David's role as the father of both

Amnon and Absalom as well as his public account-
ability as king of Israel.

READ 2 SAMUEL 14:1-24.

✐ 2.   What was Joab's strategy to end Absalom's exile?

Why do you think Joab did this?

3.   What did David's restrictions on Absalom reveal?

Do you think David's decision was wise or unwise? Why?

Read 2 Samuel 14:25-33.

4. What is your impression of Absalom as he is described here?

5. What do these verses, as well as the willingness of the Tekoan woman to tell her story to King David, say about Israel's general attitude toward Absalom?

6. Why did Absalom resort to such destructive measures to bring his case before his father?

What indications of his frustrations and the intensity of his feelings do you find in this passage?

7. At the time Absalom and David reconciled, what seemed to be Absalom's attitude when he came before his father the king?

What was David's attitude?

8. How did David's series of decisions concerning his son's fate lay the foundation for Absalom's later rebellion in 2 Samuel 15?

9. Discuss how the ordinary decisions we make every day can have far-reaching effects in our lives, our families, and even our world. Describe a personal example if you can.

READ LUKE 15:11-24.

10. Compare and contrast the homecoming of Absalom and the prodigal son. In what ways are David and the father in the story of the prodigal similar?

In what ways are they different?

11. What has this passage taught you about the importance of dealing wisely with your own family situations? Describe a current family situation in which you need to seek God's wisdom.

12. What steps can you take to develop stronger relationships within your family?

How Do I Respond to God's Judgment?

2 SAMUEL 15:1–16:14

Centuries ago, John Bunyan, the author of *Pilgrim's Progress,* wrote:

He that is down needs fear no fall.
He that is low no pride.
He that is humble ever shall
Have God to be his guide.

It's often when we are at our lowest that we see ourselves as we really are. Such was the case for King David at this time in his life. As Nathan had prophesied, evil arose against David from his own household. One son had been killed and another son was turning against him—both events the devastating result of David's own sin and inaction. God had forgiven David, but David continued to experience the consequences of his sin. Feeling the weight of God's judgment, David humbled himself and trusted God for the future.

1. Describe a time when you have experienced the consequences of sin in your life or have seen its consequences in someone else's life.

READ 2 SAMUEL 15:1-12.

2. Describe Absalom's politics.

⚘ 3. What had Absalom accomplished in four years (verses 6-10)?

✍ 4. What plans had Absalom made? What do you think motivated his rebellion?

READ 2 SAMUEL 15:13-37.

5. Why did David decide to leave the city (verse 14)?

✍ 6. In what ways did David try to release Ittai and the Gittites from the obligation of following him?

How would Ittai's response have helped David at this time of personal upheaval?

7. What did the backing of the Levites indicate?

8. Why did David want the Levites to take the ark back to Jerusalem?

If David doubted that God would continue to bless him, why do you think he placed himself completely in God's hands?

9. How did Hushai express his support for David (verse 32)?

What kind of help did David ask Hushai to provide (verses 34-36)?

Read 2 Samuel 16:1-14.

✐ 10. Of what did Ziba accuse Mephibosheth?

11. After losing many of his supporters, what further criticism did David have to face (verses 5-8)?

12. Looking at the entire passage, what evidence do you see that David was aware that he was receiving God's judgment?

How did this awareness affect David's posture toward God?

13. If possible, describe a time in your life when sin's effects have brought you down. During such a time, how did you relate to God? What can you learn from David's response to the multiplied adversity of sin?

How Do I Show Mercy?

2 SAMUEL 16:15–18:33

If grace is getting the "good" we *don't* deserve, mercy is *not* getting all the "bad" we *do* deserve. Children don't understand the statement "This hurts me more than it hurts you" until they become parents. Then they know the deep pain parents experience when their children rebel and must be disciplined. Wise parents understand the importance of including both mercy and grace in dealing with their children.

The rebellion of Absalom brought personal pain to David as a father as well as political chaos to his kingdom. But David had learned that God's discipline in his life was always mixed generously with love, and, as a result, he was able to offer the same sort of mercy to his son.

1. How do you define *mercy?*

READ 2 SAMUEL 16:15–17:29.

2. What did Hushai, David's friend, do to gain the confidence of Absalom (16:16-19)?

✎ 3. Compare Absalom's activity in 16:22 with Nathan's prophecy in 2 Samuel 12:11-12.

4. What did Hushai do to thwart Ahithophel's plan (17:7-10)?

5. Summarize the suspenseful spy story in 17:15-22. Why do you think Ahithophel responded as he did (verse 23)?

6. What ministry did the three friends fulfill for David and his people (17:27-29)?

READ 2 SAMUEL 18.

7. How did David organize his army?

8. What did David's request for Absalom reveal about how David felt about his son (verse 5)?

✐ 9. What reasons did Joab have for disregarding David's wishes concerning Absalom?

10. How did David's reaction to Absalom's death differ from that of his loyal followers and the army? Why?

11. David was prepared for war, but he spoke with love and was ready to show mercy to Absalom. What experiences had taught David mercy?

12. In what ways does God's mercy in your life affect your relationships with others?

Can I Exhibit Loyalty?

2 SAMUEL 19–20

With Absalom dead and his army defeated, there was nothing standing in the way of David's return to Jerusalem. But would the people of Israel welcome his return?

God's mercy for David continued during this time of uncertainty. Several individuals crossed David's path. Some he could trust, and others he couldn't. In this study we'll see the benefits David experienced from loyal friends. Even though the circumstances are centuries away from ours, it is still important to have friends you can count on.

1. Would you say your family is a loyal one? If you wish, explain why or why not.

READ 2 SAMUEL 19.

2. Consumed with grief, what did David fail to acknowledge?

3. How did God show mercy toward David through Joab?

⚘ 4. What opinions did the Israelites and the men of Judah have concerning David's return?

5. Do you think David's decision to promote Amasa, Absalom's commander, was wise or unwise? Why?

✎ 6. What motive was behind Shimei's words in verses 19-20? (Review 2 Samuel 16:5-8.)

✎ 7. What did Mephibosheth do to demonstrate his allegiance to the king (verses 24,27-28,30)?

What do we learn in this passage about Ziba, Saul's steward?

8. Barzillai had been a supporter of David when he fled from Absalom. How did Barzillai offer help to David at this time (verse 37)?

Kimham was Barzillai's son. Why might this gift
have been of particular comfort to David?

✐ 9. Discuss how the conflict described in verses 40-43
was partly due to David's impatience in 19:11-12.

READ 2 SAMUEL 20.

10. What did Sheba do to aggravate the conflict
between Judah and Israel?

11. What evidences do you see of David's reestablishing
himself as king (verses 3-6)?

12. Why was Amasa killed? What action united Joab's troops with those of the slain Amasa (verses 10-13)?

13. What are your impressions of the discourse between Joab and the wise woman?

14. Throughout this time of upheaval, what individuals had David been able to trust?

How had they shown their loyalty?

15. In what situations are you called to be loyal?

What can you do to demonstrate your loyalty?

We will omit the study of 2 Samuel 21, which describes a situation that most scholars believe took place early in David's reign, most probably a short time after the conquest of Jerusalem. This chapter relates various problems David faced in his reign including a famine, dealings with the kinsmen of Saul, and a lengthy war with the Philistines. To continue the narrative of David's life, we will first study 2 Samuel 24 and 1 Kings 1–2 and then return to 2 Samuel 22–23.

Is God My Security?

2 SAMUEL 24

It's easy enough to trust God when everything is going smoothly and we feel in control of our lives. But can we trust him when tragic events happen or when we feel vulnerable? While David was recovering from Absalom's revolt and the attempted insurrection of Sheba, he tried to regain control of his kingdom by making sure he had a strong army. It may seem normal for a king to operate this way, but it revealed something about David's faith at the time. As we read about how God tested David's character and punished Israel, we'll see that humans tend to judge things by their present appearance, while God sees the ultimate consequences.

1. When is it most difficult for you to trust God?

✍ READ 2 SAMUEL 24:1-10.

✍ 2. What seemed to be David's motivation for taking a census?

Whom did David *not* seek out for guidance or counsel before taking the census?

3. Contrast what David may have personally expected to achieve by this military census with what he experienced after the counting was completed (verse 10).

4. Discuss a time when you worked to get something you believed would give you satisfaction or security and were sorely disappointed after you got it. Where do you need to find your security and satisfaction?

READ 2 SAMUEL 24:11-25.

5. After David confessed his sin, what terrible message did the prophet Gad deliver?

6. What did David's answer indicate about his faith (verse 14)?

7. How did God's judgment completely undermine what David had hoped to achieve by the registration?

8. What was David willing to sacrifice in verse 17?

How did God show his mercy to David?

9. What does David's reply to Araunah teach us about the kind of offering God wants?

What can you do to offer "sacrifices" to God that cost you something? Be specific.

10. How might prayer have helped David when he felt insecure and vulnerable?

11. How can prayer help you become more dependent on God for your security and satisfaction?

How Would God Describe My Life?

2 SAMUEL 22:1–23:7

Sören Kierkegaard said that life must be lived forward but can only be understood backward. As David looked back at the end of his life, he could see God's gracious work and praised him for it. David had sinned greatly, but he had also known God's faithfulness and the completeness of his forgiveness. Because of this, David was free to grow in his relationship with God and to call others to know the God he loved so much.

1. If God were to write an obituary for you, what would you want him to write?

✍ READ 2 SAMUEL 22:1-20.

2. How many times did David use the words "me" or "my" in verses 2-3? What does this reflect about David's relationship with God?

How would you evaluate your current level of dependence on God for protection and deliverance?

3. Describe the severity of David's plight in verses 5-6. What was his response to this hardship?

4. What was God's response to David's call for help (verses 17-20)?

How has God answered your cries for help in the middle of a desperate situation?

READ 2 SAMUEL 22:21-37.

✎ 5. What reason did David give for God's intervention on his behalf?

List all the words that describe or are related to David's right position toward God.

6. If possible, give some examples of God's enablement and strengthening in your life that parallel David's experience in this passage.

In what ways does God "broaden" your path (verse 37)?

READ 2 SAMUEL 22:38-51.

7. How do these verses illustrate David's perseverance and unswerving allegiance to God?

8. How did the awareness that "the Lord lives" (verse 47) help David be obedient?

9. How do you know the Lord lives?

In what ways does this confidence aid your obedience, praise, and witness?

✐ READ 2 SAMUEL 23:1-7.

10. What roles did David use to describe himself in verse 1?

11. What words did God use to characterize David's reign? his character?

12. Reread verse 5. In Jesus Christ, the son of David, is found the fulfillment of the everlasting covenant of salvation, life, and peace between God and his people. How is your life "arranged and secured" because of this?

Between now and the next study, write a psalm of your own that reflects your life with the Lord right now. Share it with someone in your study group, your pastor, or a friend.

Do I Know the Secret of Success?

1 KINGS 1:1–2:12

David continued to reign as a merciful and just king for the remainder of his life. Scripture records his life with candor, revealing his triumphs and trials, his sinful waywardness and his faithful obedience. He wasn't perfect, but he lived with an open heart toward God, and he was blessed when he obeyed God. As David faced trouble near the end of his life, he once again had to lean on God for help and strength, and he was able to pass on some valuable advice to his son.

1. What is one important piece of advice you would want to pass on to your children (or nephews, nieces, or the children of close friends)?

✒ READ 1 KINGS 1.

2. What was Adonijah's ambition (verse 5)?

    In what ways might David's lack of parental
    discipline (verse 6) have contributed to Adonijah's
    attitude and behavior?

3. Who joined Adonijah in the conspiracy? Who was
    excluded from Adonijah's party (verses 7-10)? Why?

4. How did David learn about Adonijah's attempt to
    seize the throne?

5. From where did David draw the determination and
    courage to face this last crisis of his life (verse 29)?

✒ 6. Who helped David install Solomon as king?

What did David do to affirm Solomon in this new role as king?

7. What was the reaction of Adonijah and his guests (verse 49)?

What protection did Adonijah hope to find by holding on to the horns of the altar?

READ 1 KINGS 2:1-12.

8. What secrets of success did David share with Solomon?

9. As he handed over the responsibilities of state to Solomon, David was aware of some unfinished business as well as unpunished wrongs and kindnesses that needed to be remembered. What trait in Solomon did David recognize and trust in dealing with these matters?

IN SUMMARY

10. As you reflect on your study of David, what aspect of his life has affected you the most? Why?

11. What have you learned from this study that has influenced your attitudes toward God as well as your commitment to him? Be as specific as possible.

12. Acts 13:22 records that when God made David king, he testified: "I have found David son of Jesse a man after my own heart; he will do everything I want him to do." What does it mean to be a person "after God's own heart"?

    What can you do that will help you become more like this?

Close with a time of prayer, asking God to help you follow him wholeheartedly.

How Does God See Me?

PSALM 139

King David was a gifted musician who was known as Israel's "singer of songs." One of his most poignant poetic expressions is found in Psalm 139, where he ponders God's intimate knowledge of us and his infinite care. It's incredible that the mighty God who created the vast universe also knows our names.

1. Describe a time when you have been particularly aware of the immensity of God's "all-knowing-ness" (omniscience).

READ PSALM 139:1-12.

2. List some specific things God knows about you. When you realize how thorough God's knowledge of you is, what is your reaction?

3. Is the knowledge of God's presence comforting to you? Why or why not?

4. How did David describe the fact that God is everywhere?

When and how have you attempted to get away
from God and his demands?

5. To what kind of "darkness" do you think David was
referring in verses 11-12?

How do we know God is adequate for any degree of
darkness?

READ PSALM 139:13-18.

6. Rewrite verses 13-16 in your own words and discuss
their significance.

7. What effect do the truths in verses 13-16 have on your confidence in God's love for you?

8. Summarize David's reaction to God's knowledge of him (verses 17-18).

How could this knowledge affect you first thing in the morning? What impact could this knowledge have on your worship, your work, and your witness in the world?

Read Psalm 139:19-24.

9. Whom have the wicked wronged? What have they done?

   Why did David hate the wicked?

10. Is this kind of righteous anger warranted in our world today? If so, against what or whom?

11. What is the difference between hating sin and hating the sinner?

How can the strong emotion of anger help you fight the effects of sin?

12. After David considered the thoughts and actions of the wicked, what did he ask of God (verses 23-24)?

13. Compare verses 23-24 with verse 1. Why do we need to ask God to search our hearts if he knows everything already?

In closing, read aloud verses 23-24 in unison as your heartfelt prayer.

Leader's Notes

STUDY 1: IS MY WORSHIP GENUINE?

Question 2. For the past sixty years, including all of Saul's reign, the ark had been resting at Ballejudah, a town bordering Philistia (see map at the beginning of this studyguide). The ark of the covenant, or ark of the testimony, held the Ten Commandments and was a sign of God's presence among the people of Israel. (See Exodus 37:1-9; 40:20-21.) It also symbolized God's power over Israel's enemies. When the Israelites came to the banks of the Jordan River, the priests carrying the ark went ahead. When their feet touched the river, the water backed up. Later, when the walls of Jericho had fallen, the priests carrying the ark on their shoulders again led the procession.

Question 8. An *ephod* was a linen loincloth worn in worship.

STUDY 2: DO I SEE FROM GOD'S PERSPECTIVE?

Question 2. The prophet Nathan was Samuel's successor.

Question 3. The Hebrew word for *dwelling* (2 Samuel 7:6) implies a place of temporary residence. God did not want a permanent house until Israel settled someplace.

Question 5. The prophecy in 2 Samuel 7:12-16 is later fulfilled to some degree in Solomon but is only completely fulfilled in Jesus Christ (see Matthew 1:1).

STUDY 3: DO I ACT WITH JUSTICE AND RIGHTEOUSNESS?

Question 3. Following David's reign, the administration of justice and righteousness quickly and almost completely disappeared in the kingdom. In fact, one concern common to all the Old Testament prophets was the lack of justice and righteousness among God's people. Israel's idolatry, the resulting oppression of her own poor, and the prevalence of corporate injustice was what eventually brought about the devastating judgment of God upon the nation.

Question 5. See 1 Samuel 20:15-17 for David's promises to Jonathan and Saul. "The account [of Mephibosheth] is intended to show how David was mindful of the duties of gratitude and loving fidelity, even when he reached the highest point of his regal authority and glory. The date when this occurred was about the middle of David's reign, as we may see from the fact that Mephibosheth, who was five years old when Saul died (2 Samuel 4:4), had a young son at the time (9:12)" (Keil and Delitzsch, *Old Testament Commentaries,* vol. 2, Grand Rapids, Mich.: Eerdmans, 1971, p. 270).

STUDY 5: CAN I REJOICE?

Note on Psalm 32. David wrote this psalm as he struggled with God after his sins of adultery and murder recorded in 2 Samuel 11.

Question 7. The Hebrew poetry of the psalms is characterized by different forms of parallelism. In Psalm 32:8, the second half of the verse is a parallel to the first, repeating and emphasizing the truth of God's guidance and care.

STUDY 6: HOW CAN I BEST LOVE MY FAMILY?

Question 2. Absalom was David's third-born son, and after Amnon's murder, he became the oldest living son. (David's second-born son, not mentioned after his birth, may have died in infancy.) Absalom was thus favored as successor to the throne, and Joab may have been trying to curry favor with the future king.

STUDY 7: HOW DO I RESPOND TO GOD'S JUDGMENT?

Question 3. Most versions render the time period in 2 Samuel 15:7 as four years rather than forty.

Question 4. Hebron was David's capital city before he captured Jerusalem. See 2 Samuel 2:1-4.

Question 6. The six hundred Gittites led by Ittai were the same band of valiant men who had been with David during the years he subdued Israel's neighbors. See 1 Samuel 23:13; 25:13; 30:1,9.

Question 10. For background on Ziba, see 2 Samuel 9. Later we will learn that Ziba abandoned Mephibosheth when David fled Jerusalem. The scheming Ziba had come to use David's difficult circumstances to his own advantage.

STUDY 8: HOW DO I SHOW MERCY?

Question 3. This act would have been a great insult to David.

Question 9. Second Samuel 18:18 states that Absalom had no heir. His three sons mentioned in 2 Samuel 14:27 must have died in infancy. This may have been one reason he tried to seize the throne. He could easily have been passed over as David's successor since he had no heir.

STUDY 9: CAN I EXHIBIT LOYALTY?

Question 4. Although Israel was a kingdom united under David, it consisted of twelve separate tribes that were fairly independent. David was from the larger clan of Judah, and Israel consisted of the remaining group of eleven northern tribes. See Numbers 26 for a listing of the Israelites by clan.

Question 6. Although David promised not to kill Shimei, he later told Solomon to offer no mercy to this treacherous adversary.

Question 7. Mephibosheth showed the traditional expressions of mourning.

Question 9. One cannot overstate the seriousness of the rift between Judah and the rest of Israel. Later, after Solomon's reign ended, the two factions were permanently divided into two separate kingdoms. Each was ruled by its own kings and maintained independent political and religious activity.

Question 12. Some group members may be put off by the violent details of revenge and war throughout 2 Samuel. If this issue is raised, it may be good to remind the group that these were historical events and reflected the culture of David's day.

We must keep the context in mind and not judge the methods by today's cultural standards. War and revenge remain a part of our world and though our weapons may seem more sophisticated, the results are nevertheless just as brutal.

Study 10: Is God My Security?

Note on 2 Samuel 24:1-10. "To the modern reader it is far from clear why it was sinful to hold a census; and if it was, it disturbs him afresh that God Himself should have prompted the sinful act. It must be allowed, first of all, that God's anger against Israel (24:1) will not have been due to some arbitrary whim. God's reasons for action are not always revealed.... This writer recognizes the overruling hand of God, whereas the later historian was more interested in the mode of the incitement, namely Satanic tempting (see 1 Chronicles 21:1)" (D. Guthrie and J. A. Motyer, eds., *New Bible Commentary: Revised,* Grand Rapids, Mich.: Eerdmans, 1970, p. 314).

Question 2. David's purpose for the census would have been to enhance the reorganization of the military and labor groups and thus get the greatest military advantage he could. The sin in this is generally believed to be one of pride and arrogance as well as misplaced trust and security.

Question 9. The Bible teaches that God is more concerned about the attitude of our hearts toward him than empty ritual. David had reflected on this earlier in his life: "The sacrifices of God are a broken spirit; a broken and contrite heart, O God, you will not despise" (Psalm 51:17).

STUDY 11: HOW WOULD GOD DESCRIBE MY LIFE?

Note on 2 Samuel 22. This psalm (revised slightly as Psalm 18) was written when David was newly established on the throne. It is placed here to celebrate the end of David's life with a song of victory and triumph. This chapter provides an outline of how God makes himself known to his people, calls them to himself, and keeps them close to him.

Question 5. In the Old Testament, good works (including sacrifices) were an *evidence* of faith and *looked forward* to the day of God's final redemption in the work of the promised Messiah. This redemption was accomplished in the death of Jesus, God's Son, on the cross of Calvary. Since that time, good works are a *response* of faith *looking back* to Jesus, the final sacrifice.

Note on 2 Samuel 23. This chapter, written at the end of David's life, completed his reflections on God's purposes. In today's world, as in David's, we must discover and define what it means to be people "after God's own heart," determined to bring him delight by our love and obedience (2 Samuel 22:20).

STUDY 12: DO I KNOW THE SECRET OF SUCCESS?

Note on 1 Kings 1. First Kings 1:1-2 presents David as an elderly man. The acquisition of a young virgin as a nurse for an elderly man was customary practice in cultures where polygamy was commonly accepted.

Question 6. To ride on the king's mule was a sign of being the appointed successor to the throne. This beginning of a dynasty was particularly meaningful for Israel since it was the first time that a king's son had come to the throne.

Question 7. The horns of the altar were projections that looked like horns and were part of the frame of the altar where burnt offerings were made (Exodus 27:2). A person seeking sanctuary might hold on to these horns (see 1 Kings 1:50-51).

What Should We Study Next?

To help your group answer that question, we've listed the Fisherman studyguides by category so you can choose your next study.

TOPICAL STUDIES

Angels by Vinita Hampton Wright

Becoming Women of Purpose by Ruth Haley Barton

Building Your House on the Lord: Marriage and Parenthood by Steve and Dee Brestin

The Creative Heart of God: Living with Imagination by Ruth Goring

Discipleship: The Growing Christian's Lifestyle by James and Martha Reapsome

Doing Justice, Showing Mercy: Christian Actions in Today's World by Vinita Hampton Wright

Encouraging Others: Biblical Models for Caring by Lin Johnson

The End Times: Discovering What the Bible Says by E. Michael Rusten

Examining the Claims of Jesus by Dee Brestin

Friendship: Portraits in God's Family Album by Steve and Dee Brestin

The Fruit of the Spirit: Growing in Christian Character by Stuart Briscoe

Great Doctrines of the Bible by Stephen Board

Great Passages of the Bible by Carol Plueddemann

Great Prayers of the Bible by Carol Plueddemann

Growing Through Life's Challenges by James and Martha Reapsome

Guidance & God's Will by Tom and Joan Stark

Heart Renewal: Finding Spiritual Refreshment by Ruth Goring

Higher Ground: Steps Toward Christian Maturity by Steve and Dee Brestin

Images of Redemption: God's Unfolding Plan Through the Bible by Ruth Van Reken

Integrity: Character from the Inside Out by Ted Engstrom and Robert Larson

Lifestyle Priorities by John White

Marriage: Learning from Couples in Scripture by R. Paul and Gail Stevens

Miracles by Robbie Castleman

One Body, One Spirit: Building Relationships in the Church by Dale and Sandy Larsen

The Parables of Jesus by Gladys Hunt

Parenting with Purpose and Grace by Alice Fryling

Prayer: Discovering What the Bible Says by Timothy Jones and Jill Zook-Jones

The Prophets: God's Truth Tellers by Vinita Hampton Wright

Proverbs and Parables: God's Wisdom for Living by Dee Brestin

Satisfying Work: Christian Living from Nine to Five by R. Paul Stevens and Gerry Schoberg

Senior Saints: Growing Older in God's Family by James and Martha Reapsome

The Sermon on the Mount: The God Who Understands Me
by Gladys Hunt
Spiritual Gifts by Karen Dockrey
Spiritual Hunger: Filling Your Deepest Longings by Jim and
Carol Plueddemann
A Spiritual Legacy: Faith for the Next Generation by Chuck
and Winnie Christensen
Spiritual Warfare by A. Scott Moreau
The Ten Commandments: God's Rules for Living by Stuart
Briscoe
Ultimate Hope for Changing Times by Dale and Sandy
Larsen
Who Is God? by David P. Seemuth
Who Is Jesus? In His Own Words by Ruth Van Reken
Who Is the Holy Spirit? by Barbara Knuckles and Ruth Van
Reken
Wisdom for Today's Woman: Insights from Esther by Poppy
Smith
Witnesses to All the World: God's Heart for the Nations
by Jim and Carol Plueddemann
Women at Midlife: Embracing the Challenges by Jeanie
Miley
Worship: Discovering What Scripture Says by Larry Sibley

BIBLE BOOK STUDIES

Genesis: Walking with God by Margaret Fromer and
Sharrel Keyes
Exodus: God Our Deliverer by Dale and Sandy Larsen
Ruth: Relationships That Bring Life by Ruth Haley Barton

Ezra and Nehemiah: A Time to Rebuild by James Reapsome
(For Esther, see Topical Studies, *Wisdom for Today's Woman*)
Job: Trusting Through Trials by Ron Klug
Psalms: A Guide to Prayer and Praise by Ron Klug
Proverbs: Wisdom That Works by Vinita Hampton Wright
Ecclesiastes: A Time for Everything by Stephen Board
Song of Songs: A Dialogue of Intimacy by James Reapsome
Jeremiah: The Man and His Message by James Reapsome
Jonah, Habakkuk, and Malachi: Living Responsibly
    by Margaret Fromer and Sharrel Keyes
Matthew: People of the Kingdom by Larry Sibley
Mark: God in Action by Chuck and Winnie Christensen
Luke: Following Jesus by Sharrel Keyes
John: The Living Word by Whitney Kuniholm
Acts 1–12: God Moves in the Early Church by Chuck and
    Winnie Christensen
Acts 13–28, see *Paul* under Character Studies
Romans: The Christian Story by James Reapsome
1 Corinthians: Problems and Solutions in a Growing Church
    by Charles and Ann Hummel
Strengthened to Serve: 2 Corinthians by Jim and Carol
    Plueddemann
Galatians, Titus, and Philemon: Freedom in Christ
    by Whitney Kuniholm
Ephesians: Living in God's Household by Robert Baylis
Philippians: God's Guide to Joy by Ron Klug
Colossians: Focus on Christ by Luci Shaw
Letters to the Thessalonians by Margaret Fromer and
    Sharrel Keyes
Letters to Timothy: Discipleship in Action by Margaret
    Fromer and Sharrel Keyes

Hebrews: Foundations for Faith by Gladys Hunt

James: Faith in Action by Chuck and Winnie Christensen

1 and 2 Peter, Jude: Called for a Purpose by Steve and Dee
    Brestin

How Should a Christian Live? 1, 2, and 3 John by Dee
    Brestin

Revelation: The Lamb Who Is a Lion by Gladys Hunt

BIBLE CHARACTER STUDIES

Abraham: Model of Faith by James Reapsome

David: Man After God's Own Heart by Robbie Castleman

Elijah: Obedience in a Threatening World by Robbie
    Castleman

Great People of the Bible by Carol Plueddemann

Men Like Us: Ordinary Men, Extraordinary God by Paul
    Heidebrecht and Ted Scheuermann

Moses: Encountering God by Greg Asimakoupoulos

Paul: Thirteenth Apostle (Acts 13–28) by Chuck and
    Winnie Christensen

Women Like Us: Wisdom for Today's Issues by Ruth Haley
    Barton

Women Who Achieved for God by Winnie Christensen

Women Who Believed God by Winnie Christensen